GW01246499

Original title:

Starlight on Ice

Author: Swan Charm

ISBN HARDBACK: 978-9908-52-014-8

ISBN PAPERBACK: 978-9908-52-015-5

ISBN EBOOK: 978-9908-52-016-2

Shimmering Nightfall

Stars awaken in the dark,
Whispers of the evening spark.
Moonlight spills on quiet paths,
Softly dancing, nature laughs.

Shadows stretch and softly creep,
While the world begins to sleep.
Crickets chirp in rhythmic tune,
Beneath the watchful silver moon.

Clouds drift gently through the night,
Draped in veils of soft twilight.
Fireflies flicker, bright and free,
Glowing gems of mystery.

The breeze carries scents so sweet,
As night's magic draws us near.
Dreams take flight on gentle wings,
In the calm, the heartstrings sing.

Wrapped in calm, the world feels light,
In this tranquil, shimmering night.
Time stands still in muted grace,
Embraced by darkness, we find our place.

Glacial Dances Under the Cosmos

Icicles hang with a crystal grace,
Reflecting starlight in their embrace.
Whirlwinds swirl across the ice,
Nature twirls, a silent slice.

The moon's glow paints a scene so bright,
As glaciers glide in the quiet night.
Stars like diamonds pierce the air,
Glistening jewels, beyond compare.

Drifting snowflakes softly fall,
Carpet of white, a blanket call.
In this world, so stark and grand,
Life in frozen forms will stand.

Echoes linger in the chill,
Frozen landscapes, beauty still.
In this dance, all time stands still,
Underneath the vast, cosmic thrill.

Sculptures born of wind and frost,
In this haven, nothing's lost.
Hearts will warm as cold creates,
Glacial beauty captivates.

Frozen Radiance

In the stillness, crystal lights,
Flickering softly through the nights.
Winter's breath, a gentle sigh,
Radiance painted 'neath the sky.

Snowflakes dance like fleeting dreams,
Whirling softly in moonbeam streams.
The world's a canvas, pure and bright,
A masterpiece of frozen light.

Glinting pools of icy glass,
Reflect the stars as moments pass.
Time seems lost in chilly grace,
Yet warmth is found in every space.

Silent woods in winter's keep,
Colors fade, but memories seep.
Through the cold, a spark remains,
A frozen heart that loves and pains.

With each sunrise, the ice will melt,
Yet frozen beauty will be felt.
In every shard, a story told,
Of frozen radiance, bold and old.

Heavenly Glint on Frigid Waters

Ripples shimmer on the lake,
Whispers soft, the night will wake.
Stars reflect on icy flow,
A dancing light, a gentle glow.

Moonbeams kiss the water's skin,
As the world breathes deep within.
Frigid waves in calm repose,
Carry secrets only night knows.

Heavenly glint on chilly streams,
Where silence wraps our truest dreams.
The heart beats soft against the cold,
In this tale, a warmth unfolds.

Froze and flowing, time stands still,
Nature's pulse, a tranquil thrill.
Beneath the stars, in awe we float,
On frigid waters, dreams will coat.

In the hush, we find a way,
To cherish light in darkened play.
The night is magic, pure and true,
In heavenly glint, we come anew.

Glacial Radiance

In the stillness of night, a shimmer,
Icicles hang in moonlit splendor.
Beneath the stars, the cold glows bright,
A beauty carved from purest winter.

Frost bites softly at the skin,
Yet warmth lingers where hearts begin.
Each breath a cloud, a fleeting trace,
In glacial radiance, find your place.

A whisper echoes through the trees,
As icy winds dance with such ease.
Glistening paths, a silent art,
Where nature paints with a gentle heart.

Light cascades on a frozen lake,
Reflections shimmer, stillness breaks.
Nature's canvas, vast and wide,
Casts a spell, drawing all inside.

In thoughts of warmth, we find our peace,
As glacial visions never cease.
With every heartbeat, every glance,
We're touched by winter's timeless dance.

Twinkling Beneath the Chill

Stars beckon from the velvet sky,
Sprinkled gently, they wink and sigh.
Each twinkle tells of tales untold,
Whispers of dreams in the night so bold.

Below the frost, the world lies still,
Nature bows to the winter's will.
Yet in the hush, a magic stirs,
Awakening hearts, it's bliss that purrs.

Moonlight drapes a silver shawl,
Cocooning silence, enchanting all.
In the chill, there's warmth to find,
As stars illuminate the wandering mind.

Each breath a cloud, a fleeting gift,
In twilight's glow, our spirits lift.
Twinkling softly, the heavens call,
Reminding us, we're part of it all.

With every heartbeat, we feel alive,
In the cold embrace, our dreams thrive.
Forever twinkling, beneath the chill,
The cosmos whispers, our hearts to fill.

Aurora's Touch

Dancing lights across the night,
Colors swirl, a wondrous sight.
In whispered greens and pinks they play,
Aurora's touch, a night ballet.

With every wave, the heavens sing,
Filling the soul, a vibrant spring.
As nature paints with hues so bold,
A tale of beauty in colors told.

Beneath this glow, the silence fades,
In awe we stand, where magic wades.
A fleeting moment, forever dear,
In auroral grace, we find no fear.

The chill of night, a welcomed friend,
With every breath, the colors blend.
Skyward glances stir the heart,
In aurora's touch, we never part.

So let us dance beneath this light,
In the vast canvas of the night.
For in this realm, our spirits soar,
In aurora's touch, forevermore.

Frigid Fantasia

In the hush of a starry night,
Winter weaves a cocoon of white.
Dreams drift softly on frosty air,
In frigid fantasia, hearts lay bare.

Crystal whispers, the world holds still,
As snowflakes twirl on winter's will.
Each path we tread, a secret maze,
Wrapped in the softest frosty daze.

Lights aglow in homes so warm,
Welcoming souls from winter's charm.
Laughter mingles, dances free,
In this grand ball of harmony.

Cold winds blow, but we are near,
Embraced by love, we shed the fear.
In every flake, a wish we cast,
In frigid fantasia, moments last.

So gather close, in winter's grace,
United here, in this sacred space.
As frost paints stories on each tree,
In frigid fantasia, let it be.

Silver Veil

In the moonlight's soft embrace,
Whispers dance upon the lace.
Veils of silver softly flow,
Hiding secrets from below.

Stars above like diamonds gleam,
Night unfolds a gentle dream.
Silver trails on paths unseen,
Magic weaves where hearts convene.

Glistening in the midnight air,
Every breath a silent prayer.
Through the shadows, spirits glide,
In this world, we step inside.

Echoes of a fleeting sigh,
Painted softly by the sky.
As the dawn begins to break,
Silver dreams begin to wake.

In the shimmer of the morn,
New horizons, life reborn.
Beneath the veil, the story stays,
Silver threads in endless plays.

Frosted Reverie

In winter's grasp, a world so bright,
Frosted dreams in purest white.
Whispers of a crystal song,
In this realm, we all belong.

Branches glisten with icy grace,
Nature wears a soft embrace.
Glistening paths where silence lingers,
Touch the frost with tender fingers.

Moonlit nights and starry skies,
Paint the canvas where time flies.
Every flake a fleeting thought,
In this wonder, warmth is sought.

Through the chill, our spirits soar,
Finding beauty at the core.
Frosted reveries paint our night,
As we dance in pure delight.

When dawn breaks with colors bold,
Stories of the night unfold.
In the heart of winter's game,
Frosted dreams will call your name.

Enchanted Nightfall

As the sun begins to fade,
Magic cloaks the evening glade.
Whispers of the night arise,
Shadows dance beneath the skies.

Crickets sing their lullabies,
While the stars begin to rise.
Moonlight bathes the earth in glow,
Filling hearts with wondrous flow.

Winds of night carry a sigh,
Underneath the velvet sky.
Every breath, a spell we weave,
In this realm, we can believe.

Ancient tales in silence spoke,
In the warmth of twilight's cloak.
As the world turns soft and slow,
Enchanted nightfall's gentle flow.

In the stillness, dreams take flight,
Guided by the silver light.
Close your eyes and let it be,
In the night, we find the key.

Celestial Icewalker

In shadows cast by starlit grace,
An icewalker finds their place.
Footprints mark the snowy earth,
Echoes of their silent birth.

Through the crystals, whispers gleam,
In the quiet, there's a dream.
Every step, a dance of fate,
Beneath the heavens, we await.

Starry paths where wishes tread,
With each breath, a prayer unsaid.
Celestial glow lights the way,
Leading forth from night to day.

From the cosmos, colors flare,
Painting frost on winter's air.
Icewalker moves like flowing breeze,
Awakening the ancient trees.

Boundless skies and worlds collide,
Within the magic, we abide.
In their dance, the night unfolds,
Celestial tales that time upholds.

Light Upon the Glaze

A shimmer glints on frosty glass,
Awakening the dreams that pass.
With gentle warmth, the sun does rise,
A dance of light beneath the skies.

Reflections of a world anew,
Soft whispers call, the morning dew.
In every corner, warmth will trace,
The beauty found in winter's grace.

A golden hue on barren trees,
As branches sway in gentle breeze.
Each touch a spark, a tender kiss,
Transforming cold to endless bliss.

With every heart, a light shall grow,
Illuminating paths we know.
In glimmers bright, our hopes resound,
In frozen realms, our love is found.

Ethereal Fragments

Whispers float on silken air,
Fragments of dreams, beyond compare.
In twilight's hush, they softly blend,
A tapestry that won't yet end.

Shadows dance on moonlit streams,
Carrying the weight of dreams.
With every breath, they rise and fall,
Ethereal echoes call us all.

A fleeting touch, a ghostly sigh,
Beneath the stars, they quietly fly.
In silence, secrets softly weave,
Holding truths we dare believe.

Through veils of night, the visions loose,
In every heart, the soul's deduce.
These fragments shine, a guiding light,
In shadows deep, illuminating night.

Dreaming in the Cold

In quiet nights when whispers freeze,
The world's asleep, a moment's peace.
Within the chill, our thoughts take flight,
Dreaming in the velvet night.

Stars like diamonds, cold yet bright,
Illuminate our hopes in sight.
Each breath a fog, a fleeting trace,
A dance of dreams in winter's embrace.

Snowflakes twirl in playful drift,
Nature's magic, the night's sweet gift.
With every flake, a story told,
We find our hearts, forever bold.

Amidst the stillness, visions bloom,
Enveloping the night's soft gloom.
In dreams we weave, our hearts unfold,
Together warm, against the cold.

Night's Icy Canvas

The night wraps tight in icy hues,
A canvas stretched, adorned with blues.
Each star a brushstroke, bold and bright,
A masterpiece born from the night.

Frozen whispers grace the air,
As midnight's cloak weaves everywhere.
In silence deep, the world takes pause,
In icy realms without a cause.

Pale moonlight paints the snow with care,
A tranquil scene, so softly rare.
With every glimmer, shadows play,
The canvas shifts, then fades away.

Embraced by cold, the heart beats strong,
Finding solace where we belong.
In night's embrace, we walk the line,
On icy paths, our spirits shine.

Muffled Lights on Frozen Ground

Whispers of the night arise,
Underneath the starlit skies.
Frozen earth, so calm and bright,
Muffled lights in gentle flight.

Shadows dance on crystal sheets,
Echoing the silence fleets.
Winter's breath, a soft caress,
Nature's art, a sweet impress.

Footsteps crunch in tranquil snow,
Where the fleeting chill winds blow.
Each step a story to be told,
In a world of white and gold.

Frosty images unfold,
In the dark, a beauty bold.
Whirling stars in midnight's dome,
Muffled lights, a cosmic home.

Glimmers fade as dawn awakes,
In the hush, the silence breaks.
Yet in frost, the memories cling,
To the song the cold winds sing.

Radiance of a Thousand Ices

From the depths where shadows flow,
Glistening crystals start to glow.
Each facet holds a frozen dream,
Radiance caught in a silver beam.

Mighty peaks in tranquil grace,
Reflect the sun's soft, tender face.
A dance of light on cold expanse,
Nature's breath, a fleeting chance.

Echoes of the ancients call,
In the shimmer, we stand tall.
A thousand voices softly sing,
In the ice, a heartfelt ring.

Iridescent hues of blue,
Painted skies in morning dew.
Each moment sparks a solemn vow,
To cherish here, to love the now.

As the evening shadows creep,
Glow of ice, a promise deep.
Radiance beneath the stars,
A beauty wrapped in cosmic bars.

Glacial Symphony of the Cosmos

In the stillness, silence reigns,
Harmony in icy chains.
Notes of frost in twilight's breath,
Glacial tunes of life and death.

Stars align in twinkling grace,
Melodies, a timeless trace.
Each echo soft as winter's sigh,
A symphony that fills the sky.

Crystals shimmer, dance, and glide,
Whispers of the world beside.
Floating notes of ancient lore,
In the stillness, hearts explore.

Frigid winds carry the sound,
Beauty lost but always found.
In the cosmos, vast and wide,
Glacial rhythms will abide.

As night falls, the wonders grow,
Notes of ice in gentle flow.
A symphony, a cosmic choir,
In the glacial light, we aspire.

Frost-kissed Dreams

In the morning light, it glows,
Whispers of winter's soft repose.
Chilling air, a breath of peace,
A world transforms; the heart finds ease.

Fields written in frosty lace,
Nature's art, a silent grace.
Every crystal, a fleeting thought,
In this stillness, battles fought.

Beneath the sky, so vast and wide,
Mysteries in each icy stride.
Frozen lakes, secrets they keep,
In frost-kissed dreams, we gently sleep.

When night descends, stars appear,
Shimmering whispers, so near.
The moonlight dances, pure and bright,
Guiding us through the velvet night.

Awake, we wander through this scene,
In a world where hope is evergreen.
Frost-kissed dreams, forever stay,
In hearts aglow, they light the way.

Celestial Frost Over Silent Fields

A blanket of white adorns the ground,
Where silence reigns; no echo found.
Frosty breath of the early dawn,
Nature's hush, a gentle yawn.

Stars twinkle above in a velvet sea,
Wonders wrapped in cold tranquility.
Each moment fleeting, a time to breathe,
In the chill, the heart learns to seethe.

Moonbeams kiss the frozen earth,
Imbuing the night with quiet mirth.
Soft whispers weave through the trees,
In this realm, the spirit sees.

Crickets chirp their last refrain,
Cold winds hum a distant strain.
Layers of frost, a soft embrace,
In the cosmos, we find our place.

Where frost meets sky, dreams take flight,
Awakened by the stars' gentle light.
Silent fields, a canvas bright,
In celestial frost, we find our sight.

Luminous Veils of the Arctic Night

A shimmering curtain of gentle light,
Enfolds the Arctic, deep in night.
Colors dance in a boundless array,
Luminous veils that softly sway.

As frosty winds serenade the land,
The magic sparkles, bold and grand.
Each whisper echoes through the cold,
Ancient stories intertwined and old.

Underneath the brilliant display,
Hearts and spirits drift away.
Beneath the quiet, souls ignite,
In luminous veils, spirits take flight.

Frozen horizons, a world awash,
Glints of silver in a quiet slosh.
Nature's palette, rich and bright,
Wrapped in wonder, lost in light.

In the stillness, serenity yields,
To the beautiful truth that nature shields.
Veils of the Arctic, we draw near,
In luminous dreams, all is clear.

Icy Reflections of Stardust

Glistening shards on a frosty pond,
Mirrored dreams of a realm beyond.
Each ripple tells of a distant star,
Whispers of wonders from afar.

Beneath the surface, secrets hide,
Tales of cosmos' eternal tide.
In icy reflections, the universe sways,
Drawing us close in its luminous gaze.

Under the cloak of a velvet night,
Galaxies twinkle with ancient light.
Every glance at the frozen stars,
Ignites a fire, mends our scars.

Winds murmur softly; time stands still,
Chilled breath dances, a haunting thrill.
In this realm where dreams collide,
Icy reflections, our hearts confide.

In the winter's grasp, we find our way,
Navigating night, through night into day.
Icy reflections bring forth the trust,
In tender moments, igniting lust.

Icy Whispers of Nightfall

Beneath the silent moon's embrace,
Whispers drift on chilling air.
Stars twinkle in their frosty grace,
Nightfall weaves a tale so rare.

Bare branches scratch the velvet sky,
Shadows dance on glistening snow.
Nature breathes a soft, low sigh,
As winter's magic starts to flow.

Footsteps crunch on crisp white ground,
Echoes fade in misty hush.
Lost in dreams that linger 'round,
In the cold, I feel the rush.

Time slows down in icy air,
Every breath a cloud of white.
Gentle breezes weave in care,
Guiding souls through starry night.

In the stillness, secrets sleep,
Wrapped in blankets made of chill.
Icy whispers softly creep,
Binding hearts with winter's thrill.

Aurora's Dance on a Frosty Path

Dancing lights in skies so wide,
Colors swirl in frosty hues.
Nature's canvas, crisp and bright,
Awakens dreams, to chase and muse.

Rippling waves of emerald green,
Brush against the icy blue.
A wondrous sight, serene, unseen,
Calls to souls, both brave and true.

Echoes whisper on the breeze,
Stories held in winter's heart.
Underneath the swaying trees,
Magic winks; we play our part.

With each step, the frost does sing,
Crystals dance in gentle light.
Nature wraps us, like a ring,
Holding close this dream so bright.

As dawn awakens softly here,
Colors fade into the day.
Yet in hearts, the joy stays near,
For winter's magic won't decay.

Shards of Light in an Icy Realm

In the depths of winter's chill,
Shards of light break through the night.
Glistening gems on distant hill,
Nature's bounty, pure delight.

Frosty breath upon my cheek,
Whispers echo in the air.
Through the silence, soft and meek,
Mysterious wonders, rare.

Crystals sparkle, twinkle bright,
Glistening paths in moonlit glow.
Every step, a sheer delight,
Guiding dreams where shadows flow.

Branches bowed with icy grace,
Frosted kisses on each limb.
Nature's beauty finds its place,
In this realm where light won't dim.

In the stillness, hearts take flight,
Savoring the frozen air.
What a treasure, purest light,
In this icy world, so rare.

Chasing Frosted Dreams

In the quiet of the night,
Frosted dreams begin to rise.
Whispers soft, a gentle light,
Twirling under starry skies.

Breathless moments held in time,
Every sparkle catches eyes.
Nature sings a frozen rhyme,
As the moon begins to rise.

Hushed reflections on the lake,
Crystals glimmer in the dark.
Each soft whisper, hearts will wake,
Chasing dreams that leave a mark.

Through the woods, the shadows play,
Guided by the silver light.
Every step, a new ballet,
As we dance till morning's bright.

In the frosted morning glow,
Secrets held within the chill.
Chasing dreams where wild winds blow,
Hearts awaken, spirits thrill.

Enchanted Winter's Embrace

Snowflakes whisper secrets, soft and light,
Blankets of white cover the night.
Trees wear crowns of crystal sheen,
A tranquil world, serene and clean.

Fires crackle in a cozy home,
Outside, the winds of winter roam.
Footprints woven in the snow,
Guide us where the wild things go.

Pine-scented air fills the space,
Nature's wonders, every trace.
Beneath the stars, our laughter rings,
In this embrace, the joy it brings.

Frozen lakes, where shadows dance,
Winter's magic, a fleeting chance.
With every breath, the chill we chase,
In this enchanted, winter's embrace.

The Chill of Spirits

In the twilight, shadows play,
Whispers of spirits drift away.
Frosty breath, a ghostly sigh,
Cold winds tell of days gone by.

Beneath the moon's pale, silver glow,
Silent echoes, depths below.
Haunting tales the dark woods weave,
During nights that never leave.

The chill of autumn fades away,
Embracing winter's icy sway.
Glancing through the misty air,
A fleeting glimpse of what was there.

Branches bare like fingers reach,
In the stillness, spirits teach.
Through the frost, their stories stream,
In the chill, we share a dream.

Glimmering Icebound Dreams

Frozen rivers, shimmering bright,
Reflecting stars on a cold night.
In the silence, dreams take flight,
Carried softly, out of sight.

Crystalline castles glimmer and shine,
Nature's art, so pure, divine.
Each flake a wish the heart ignites,
In this stillness, wonder invites.

Through the forest, shadows glide,
With each step, they softly bide.
Frozen visions, crystal clear,
Whispers carried, oh so near.

A world encased in icy streams,
Wonderland of glimmering dreams.
Under the stars, we find our way,
In icebound forms, we long to stay.

A Dance of Light

Sunrise paints the world anew,
Colorful rays, a vibrant hue.
Joyful shadows prance around,
In this moment, hope is found.

Amidst the laughter, music flows,
A dance of light, as kindness grows.
With every twirl and every spin,
Hearts awaken, let joy in.

Glowing warm like fireside dreams,
In the meadow, sunlight beams.
Nature's rhythm, pure delight,
In the gentle touch of light.

Hand in hand, we weave our fate,
Together, we celebrate.
With every step, we unite,
In the magic of this light.

Twinkling Frost on Midnight's Canvas

Beneath the stars, the night is still,
A frost that glitters as time stands still.
Each crystal shard, a story untold,
Whispers of secrets in the dark, so bold.

The moon's soft glow paints shadows long,
While twilight hums a soothing song.
Footprints trace where silence reigns,
In winter's grasp, all beauty remains.

From trees that glisten, sparkling bright,
To the frozen pond reflecting light.
A tapestry woven with nature's thread,
On midnight's canvas, where dreams are spread.

With every breath, the air crisp and pure,
Time freezes, in its quiet allure.
A moment held, like a whispered vow,
Twinkling frost on the earth's gentle brow.

So let us dance in this winter's embrace,
Where chill and warmth find their place.
In the hush of night, let our spirits soar,
Beneath the stars, forevermore.

Chill of the Celestial Sea

Waves of chill in the moonlit tide,
Where silence sings, and shadows hide.
The ocean whispers tales of old,
Infinite depths where secrets unfold.

Stars reflected on the water's face,
Each glimmering light, a trace of grace.
The currents dance, a timeless flow,
In the chill of night, where dreams can grow.

Soft breezes carry a haunting tune,
With echoes of the silver moon.
A lullaby sung by the deep abyss,
In this tranquil world, there's no need to miss.

As tides enchanted gently rise,
Under the watch of starry skies.
The sea and night in a tender kiss,
In the chill of the celestial bliss.

So let us wander where the waves break free,
In harmony with the vast, deep sea.
Where the cold and calm forever entwine,
In the chill of the night, your hand in mine.

Winter's Glittering Symphony

A symphony plays in the frosty air,
With notes of silence, pure and rare.
Each flake a melody, soft as a sigh,
Falling gently from the leaden sky.

The world adorned in white and gray,
Beneath the canopy, dreams softly sway.
Trees stand tall, their branches bare,
Embracing the stillness everywhere.

The whisper of winds, a gentle breeze,
Carries the echoes of winter's ease.
A harmony crafted by nature's hand,
In this glittering wonderland.

Laughter echoes, kids at play,
Building snowmen in the light of day.
Joyful moments wrapped in the cold,
A symphony of life, bright and bold.

As twilight falls, the stars ignite,
Offering warmth in the winter's night.
Together we sing, hearts intertwined,
In winter's symphony, forever aligned.

Sparkle of a Thousand Worlds

In the void of space, a magic unfolds,
With the sparkle of stars, diamonds like gold.
Each blink a portal, each twinkle a dream,
A universe vast as a flowing stream.

Galaxies whirl in a cosmic dance,
Inviting us all to take a chance.
With every heartbeat, the cosmos calls,
In the silence of night, wonder befalls.

Nebulas burst in colors so bright,
A canvas painted with celestial light.
The sparkle of worlds, both near and far,
Each speck a story, each light a star.

Time and space bend in the cosmic embrace,
As we wander through this timeless place.
With eyes wide open, we seek and explore,
The sparkle of life, forevermore.

So let us journey through the stellar sea,
With dreams unbound, just you and me.
In the vastness of all, where hearts can swirl,
We'll find the sparkle of a thousand worlds.

Chilled Dimensions

In realms where whispers softly play,
The icy breath of night holds sway.
Figures dance in twilight's gleam,
Fragile moments lost in dream.

Shadows stretch with silent grace,
As stars adorn the endless space.
Every breath a frosty sigh,
Time stands still as hours fly.

Beneath the moon's soft silver thread,
Ancient tales of magic spread.
A realm where silence reigns supreme,
Awakening that dormant dream.

Echoes of a world once bright,
Fade away in muted light.
Frosted whispers weave and twine,
In this chilled, enchanted shrine.

Lost within these quiet charms,
Wrapped in nature's tender arms.
Here, the heart finds space to roam,
In chilled dimensions, we find home.

Glittering Veils

In morning's light, a shimmer gleams,
A tapestry of woven dreams.
Glittering veils of dew-kissed grass,
Whisper tales that time won't pass.

Colors burst in gentle sway,
As nature greets the waking day.
Radiant beams in playful chase,
Illuminate the quiet space.

Every leaf, a dazzling gem,
In this land where wonders stem.
Magic hides in every fold,
Stories waiting to be told.

In sunsets draped in golden hues,
Weaving patterns the heart pursues.
Glittering veils of twilight's song,
Draw us near where we belong.

Wrapped in beauty, fleeting, brief,
Life's delicate, tender brief.
Through the veils of time we move,
In this dance, our spirits prove.

Spirit of the Frost

In the chill of dawn's embrace,
The frost unveils a hidden place.
Spirit whispers, soft and clear,
Bringing nature's heart so near.

Glistening branches, white and bright,
Paint a canvas of pure light.
Each crystal spark, a shard of grace,
A moment captured in its place.

Breath visible in the crisp air,
Echoes of a world laid bare.
The spirit dances, wild and free,
On this stage of winter's spree.

With each footstep, shadows play,
As sunlight pierces through the gray.
Each turn unveils a secret born,
Crafted from the delicate morn.

Embrace the frost, the cold caress,
In this beauty, we find rest.
Spirit of the frost, we find,
Whispers of the heart, entwined.

Illuminated Serenity

In quiet nights where stars align,
The peace unfolds, a gentle sign.
Illuminated paths appear,
Guiding souls that wander near.

Softly glowing, warmth ignites,
Embracing stillness, calming sights.
Each moment, pure tranquility,
A dance of shadows, wild and free.

Whispers carried on the breeze,
Nature's secrets brought to ease.
Underneath the moon's soft glow,
Hearts entwined, a love to show.

The world slows down, a tender grace,
In illuminated, sacred space.
Every heartbeat, a soothing sound,
In this haven, joy is found.

Let your spirit freely soar,
In this peace, we seek for more.
Illuminated journeys blend,
With serenity that transcends.

Dreaming in Silver Hues

In twilight's soft embrace, we soar,
Whispers of stars, a distant lore.
Moonlight drapes the silent sea,
Crafting dreams where hearts fly free.

Gentle breezes in silver streams,
Guide us softly through our dreams.
Reflections dance on twilight's edge,
Carving paths, a glowing pledge.

Every shadow holds a light,
Glimmers hidden from our sight.
In this world where wishes bloom,
Hope ignites the darkest room.

Softly now, the night descends,
With tender whispers, time suspends.
Wrapped in silver, we take flight,
Together woven into night.

Frosty Echoes of Cosmic Murmurs

Underneath a cobalt sky,
Frosty whispers gently sigh.
The cosmos sings, a chilling tune,
Awakening the frozen moon.

Stars like diamonds gleam and dance,
In their glow, we dare to glance.
Voices echo through the night,
Tales of worlds beyond our sight.

Every heartbeat, cold and bright,
Marks the rhythm of the night.
Frosty trails on distant stars,
Map our dreams, erase our scars.

In this vastness, we explore,
In frozen moments, we adore.
Underneath the cosmic tome,
We find whispers of our home.

Wandering Lights on Slippery Paths

Beneath the glimmer of twilight's glow,
We wander paths where soft winds blow.
Guided by lights, so bright, so fair,
In this dusk, we shed our fears.

Footsteps echo on whispered trails,
Where every story gently sails.
Through tangled woods and shadows deep,
We chase the dreams that never sleep.

With slippery paths to weave and wind,
Lost in thoughts, we seek to find.
Guided by lanterns, each flickering flame,
Awakens whispers of a name.

Echoes of laughter, soft and sweet,
Remind us of each fleeting beat.
We'll follow lights, like stars above,
Finding paths in endless love.

Midnight's Gemstone Carpet

At the edge of dreams, we lay,
On a carpet where shadows play.
Midnight's jewels twinkle bright,
Guiding souls through the night.

Each gemstone tells a story true,
Of hopes and wishes, old and new.
Carried softly by the breeze,
They whisper secrets with such ease.

Underneath the velvet sky,
We find comfort, you and I.
On this canvas, dark and wide,
Every gem, a cosmic guide.

A tapestry of stars unfolds,
In midnight's arms, our dreams are rolled.
With every glimmer, hearts ignite,
On this gemstone carpet, we take flight.

Luminous Frostbite

Amidst the chill of winter's breath,
The world is draped in icy lace,
Each crystal glimmers, delicate,
A dance of light, a frozen grace.

Trees adorned with shimmering frost,
Whispers of magic fill the air,
In silver shadows, dreams are lost,
Nature's elegance laid bare.

Stars twinkle in the icy night,
Reflecting on a canvas bright,
Each flake a story, each hue a rhyme,
Frozen moments, captured time.

Footsteps crunch on paths of white,
Hearts warmed by the frosty glow,
In the stillness, pure delight,
Where silence dwells, and dreams can grow.

Beneath the moon's soft, watchful eye,
The world transforms in pale light,
In every breath, a fleeting sigh,
Life's beauty wrapped in winter's night.

Gleaming Silence

In the hush of twilight's veil,
A silence whispers, soft and deep,
The world may spin, but here we sail,
In tranquil waters, dreams we keep.

Stars remind us of distant shores,
Their twinkling echoes guide our way,
In stillness, the heart gently soars,
Through realms where night and peace do play.

The moon extends its silver hand,
Inviting all to pause and feel,
In this embrace, we understand,
The strength of silence, pure and real.

Glistening thoughts drift like the mist,
Where worries fade in gentle light,
An unseen thread, our dreams persist,
In gleaming silence, we take flight.

Time stands still, its breath in sync,
With every heartbeat, life anew,
In this moment, pause and think,
In glorious silence, me and you.

The Night's Tapestry

Sewn with whispers, stars align,
The night unfurls a sacred tale,
Constellations weave, divine design,
An ancient script, a moonlight trail.

Shadows stretch, the world serene,
In velvet skies, dreams softly play,
Each twinkle holds a hidden glean,
A tapestry of night and day.

Winds carry secrets, softly spoken,
In silence, stories drift and weave,
Each thread a bond, a promise broken,
In the fabric of night, we believe.

Crickets serenade the dusk,
While fireflies dance, a fleeting spark,
In hues of gold, the night's a musk,
An embrace that chases away the dark.

As dawn approaches with gentle grace,
The night retracts, but leaves a trace,
A memory, a fleeting glance,
In the night's tapestry, we find our chance.

Whispering Light

Morning breaks with tender glow,
As shadows stretch and dreams take flight,
In every beam, the world will know,
The gentle touch of whispering light.

Through rustling leaves, the sunlight streams,
Awakening life, both near and far,
In every heart, a dance of dreams,
Guided softly by the sun's warm star.

Threads of gold in the morning mist,
Caress the earth with loving grace,
In nature's arms, we find our tryst,
Beneath the sky's embracing face.

Each ray a promise, bright and clear,
Illuminating paths long sought,
In whispering light, we feel no fear,
For every soul is deeply caught.

As day unfolds in vibrant hues,
With open hearts, we touch the sky,
In the glow, we find our muse,
In whispering light, we learn to fly.

Glistening Dreams

In the quiet of the night,
Stars twinkle like the sea,
Whispers of a slumbered heart,
Dancing in a world that's free.

Moonlight spills upon the ground,
Casting silver shadows bright,
Every dream a spark of hope,
Floating gently, pure delight.

Thoughts take flight on gossamer,
Soaring o'er the misty clouds,
Wrapped in warmth, a soft cocoon,
Where silence sings and dreams are loud.

Gentle breezes cradle wishes,
Carrying them far away,
In this realm of endless wonder,
Tomorrow's dawn will brightly play.

With each breath, the night unfolds,
A tapestry of nightless seams,
As we drift through glimmering skies,
Chasing softly woven dreams.

Celestial Reflections

Beneath the vast, eternal dome,
Stars reflect in tranquil pools,
Whispers of the universe,
Echoing like ancient rules.

The moon, a pearl suspended high,
Guides the tides of time and fate,
In the dance of cosmic light,
We find our hopes, we contemplate.

Comets blaze like fleeting thoughts,
Across the velvet canvas wide,
Each trail a tale of longing dreams,
Journeying through the cosmic tide.

Wonders wrapped in silver hues,
Hold secrets of the night so deep,
Cradled in the arms of stars,
Where even the lost can sleep.

So, gaze upon the skies above,
Let reflections spark your mind,
In the constellations bright,
Our destinies are intertwined.

Frozen Whispers

Amidst the snow, the silence breathes,
Whispers wrapped in winter's chill,
Each flake a note, a soft refrain,
Nature's song, a tranquil thrill.

Trees adorned in frosted lace,
Stand still beneath the silver light,
Time suspends, a fleeting pause,
In the heart of the coldest night.

Footsteps crunch on crystal ground,
Echoes of a world asleep,
In this realm of frozen dreams,
Secrets lie in layers deep.

Wind carries tales from far away,
Rustling through the barren bare,
While shadows dance on icy breath,
Whispering soft, a frozen prayer.

As dawn breaks with a gentle hue,
The frost dissolves to morning's kiss,
Yet in my heart, the whispers stay,
A memory of winter's bliss.

Nightfall's Embrace

As day surrenders to the night,
Stars flicker like forgotten dreams,
In the hush, the world lies still,
Wrapped in soft, velvety seams.

Shadows stretch and dance about,
Embracing all in twilight's glow,
Every heart a beating drum,
In rhythm with the night's soft flow.

The moon, a guardian so bright,
Sheds light upon the hidden fears,
Painting shadows on the ground,
Wiping away the lingering tears.

Crickets sing their evening song,
A chorus in the cool night air,
While dreams begin their gentle flight,
In the stillness, all seems fair.

So let the darkness pull you close,
Find solace in its calm embrace,
For in the night, we are reborn,
A journey toward a tranquil place.

Chill of Echoes in Glimmering Light

Whispers float in the bright glow,
Softly dancing where shadows grow.
Each flicker tells a secret's tale,
Carried forth on a winter's gale.

Footsteps muffled in the night,
Under stars, a wondrous sight.
The chill bites through, yet warmth we find,
In echoes lost, our souls entwined.

Through the crystal air we roam,
In this silence, we feel at home.
Moments freeze, yet time will flow,
In glimmering light, our hearts will glow.

Breathless nights so far away,
Held in dreams where shadows play.
With every whisper, starlight breathes,
In the chill, our spirit weaves.

As dawn beckons, cold will wane,
But memories linger, sweet refrain.
In glimmering light, we say goodbye,
To echoes soft beneath the sky.

Starry Veils Over Icebound Plains

Beneath the moon, a silver thread,
Starry veils where dreams are spread.
In the stillness, whispers call,
Over icebound plains, we sprawl.

Every flake, a tiny spark,
Illuminates the frozen dark.
Each glimmer dances, swift and bright,
In the cold embrace of night.

Footprints fade, the past is gone,
Yet memories linger, like a song.
We wander through the crystal night,
Beneath the stars, our hearts take flight.

Dreams entwine with frosty air,
Painting visions beyond compare.
In this expanse, we feel so small,
Yet boundless in the starry thrall.

Gentle winds carry our sighs,
Caressing shadows as they rise.
With every star, our hopes align,
Over icebound plains, we find divine.

Crystalline Reflections at Dusk

Dusk arrives in shades of gray,
Crystalline reflections play.
Each shimmer glows, a fleeting blaze,
In twilight's soft and gentle haze.

Frozen rivers hold their breath,
Mirrored stillness, hinting death.
Yet life abounds in whispers low,
In this serene and lovely show.

We watch as colors slowly fade,
In the quiet, peace is laid.
With every glance, new worlds appear,
A delicate dance, soft and clear.

Nature's art in still design,
Crystalline patterns intertwine.
In dusk's embrace, our spirits soar,
Reflecting truths we've felt before.

As night unveils its velvet sheet,
We savor silence, bittersweet.
In each reflection, memories swell,
Dusk's gentle whispers weave their spell.

Ethereal Serenity on a Frosty Night

In the stillness of the frost,
Whispers linger, never lost.
Ethereal calm wraps the land,
Guiding dreams with tender hand.

Stars emerge in crystal skies,
Shimmer softly, lullabies.
Every flake that falls, a sigh,
In the hush, our spirits fly.

Moonlight dances on the snow,
Painting shadows in its glow.
Silken threads bind night and day,
In this peace, we long to stay.

Nature's breath, a gentle hush,
Inviting hearts to find the rush.
In frosty air, we feel alive,
In serenity, our dreams survive.

So let us walk this path of light,
Through frosty realms of pure delight.
With every step, we breathe anew,
In ethereal peace, our souls break through.

Stardust Dance

In whispers of the twilight haze,
Stars twirl in gentle, soft ballet.
Each twinkle paints a dreamlike phase,
As cosmic rhythms start to play.

They spin through vast, unending night,
With sparkles tracing paths of grace.
The universe a canvas bright,
Where worlds collide in silent space.

Galaxies swirl like lovers' glide,
While comets trace their fiery trails.
A dance where secrets choose to hide,
In starlit notes, the cosmos wails.

Beneath this vast celestial dome,
We join the dance, entwined in light.
With every heartbeat, we feel home,
In stardust dreams that touch the night.

So let us sway with cosmic chance,
In rhythm with the universe.
Together in this stardust dance,
Our souls entwined, forever terse.

Icy Luminescence

Beneath the frost, the world aglow,
A brilliant sheen of moonlit frost.
Each flake a gem, a shimmering show,
In night's embrace, no warmth is lost.

Shadows stretch in silver light,
While whispers chill the frozen air.
A tranquil world, so calm and bright,
Where nature breathes her frosted prayer.

Icicles hang like crystal tears,
Glistening on the eaves with pride.
In this cold space, we cast our fears,
And find the warmth that love provides.

The night unfolds a tale to tell,
Of icy blooms that softly shine.
In this mosaic, all is well,
A world transformed, pure and divine.

As warmth from heart begins to flow,
We dance beneath the silver sky.
In icy luminescence, we grow,
Two souls adorned, together high.

Moonlit Serenade

The night is draped in silver grace,
The moon casts shadows, soft and deep.
With every note, the stars embrace,
In melodies, our secrets keep.

The wind, a whisper through the trees,
Sings lullabies of dreams gone by.
Each rustle brings a gentle breeze,
As night unveils its whispered sigh.

Beneath this vast, enchanted sky,
We find a rhythm in our hearts.
With every glance, the moments fly,
In moonlit paths, where magic starts.

A serenade of love and light,
With echoes soft as velvet night.
We dance beneath the stars so bright,
Two shadows merging, hearts in flight.

In whispered dreams and fleeting time,
Our souls entwined, a sweet caress.
This moonlit serenade, sublime,
Will linger still, in tenderness.

Crystalized Night

A tapestry of shimmering dreams,
The night is dressed in crystal sheen.
Each star a point, or so it seems,
Reflecting all that might have been.

In silence, shadows softly creep,
Through fog that blankets all below.
The world is held in secrets deep,
While time does pause, a subtle show.

The ice extends its gentle touch,
To every branch, each leaf and stone.
A moment frozen, still as such,
In crystal arms, we feel at home.

The echoes of the day's delight,
Resound in quiet, tender tones.
A beauty found in dark of night,
In crystalized embrace, we're known.

So let us wander through this chill,
With hearts that dance to nature's tune.
In crystalized night, we find our thrill,
A world reborn beneath the moon.

Icy Echoes

In the silence of night, cold winds sigh,
Echoes of winter beneath the sky.
Frozen whispers in the crisp air play,
Dancing shadows as twilight fades away.

Footsteps softly step on frosted ground,
Nature's beauty in silence unbound.
A quiet serenade, soft and low,
As stars above twinkle in a row.

Branches glisten with a delicate lace,
Icy patterns in their frozen embrace.
Beneath the moon's gaze, a world so still,
Winter's breath, a tender chill.

The heart beats softly, a rhythm clear,
In this frozen realm, all we hold dear.
Icy echoes calling from afar,
Whispering secrets of the midnight star.

As dawn approaches, the frost will fade,
Leaving behind the night's cool jade.
Yet in the memory, the chill will stay,
In icy echoes, we'll find our way.

Frosted Sky

A canvas painted with hues so bright,
Frosted sky at the edge of night.
Clouds like cotton drift and gleam,
In the twilight, we lose the dream.

Colors blend in a soft embrace,
Nature's artwork, a breathtaking place.
As daylight whispers its sweet goodbye,
We gaze upon the frosted sky.

Stars awaken, twinkling gold,
Stories of old in silence told.
A silver moon begins to rise,
Casting its glow on winter's guise.

Gentle breezes carry the chill,
Nature sleeping, yet time stands still.
In the magic, our hearts shall fly,
Underneath the frosted sky.

Moments cherished, night's soft call,
Beauty captured, the world enthralled.
In dreams we wander, by and by,
Enveloped in the frosted sky.

Whispers of the Celestial

Above the world, a blanket spread,
Whispers of the celestial thread.
Stars entwined in the midnight blue,
Stories of ages shared anew.

Galaxies spinning in wondrous dance,
Inviting souls to take a chance.
Light-years echo through the endless night,
Galactic dreams, a beacon of light.

In the vastness, our fears release,
Finding solace, a moment of peace.
Nebulae painted in colors wide,
In their beauty, we take pride.

Voices of stardust softly call,
Reminding us we are part of it all.
In the silence, the universe sighs,
Whispers of hope from celestial skies.

With each twinkle, a question posed,
In cosmic wonder, our hearts enclosed.
Beneath the stars, we feel the high,
In whispers of the celestial sky.

Shining Pathways

Beneath the stars, paths shimmer bright,
Shining pathways in the velvet night.
Each step a journey, a tale untold,
With dreams alight in hues of gold.

Onward we wander, spirits alight,
With the moon guiding through the night.
Through forests deep and valleys wide,
Along shining pathways, our hopes abide.

The air sparkles with each gentle breeze,
Threads of magic dance among the trees.
Every moment, a chance to embrace,
The beauty of life in this sacred space.

With every heartbeat, the world awakes,
As dreams unfold, and stillness breaks.
In shadows cast, our fears shall die,
On shining pathways, we learn to fly.

Together we walk, hand in hand,
In this radiant, glowing land.
With love as our guide, we'll rise up high,
Finding our way on pathways that shine.

Polar Serenade of Shimmering Stars

In the stillness of the night,
Stars twinkle with delight.
Whispers of the icy breeze,
Dance among the ancient trees.

A symphony of frost and light,
Guides us through the endless night.
Moonlit paths of glimmering white,
Lead our hearts, a wondrous flight.

Shadows cast by nature's grace,
Reveal a soft and tranquil space.
Echoes of the North's refrain,
Call us to its pure domain.

Through the auroras' vibrant glow,
Gentle dreams begin to flow.
In this frozen, calm embrace,
We find a sacred, holy place.

Let the stars be our guide,
As we wander side by side.
In this serenade so bright,
Together, we conquer the night.

Gleaming Crimes of the Heart

In shadows deep, where secrets lie,
Hearts collide, and passions sigh.
Glistening tears trace silent paths,
Each moment fuels the aftermath.

Whispers sweet, yet laced with pain,
Promises lost, beneath the rain.
Desire's fire, a dangerous game,
Burning bright, yet leaving shame.

Beneath the stars, a pledge was made,
But innocence begins to fade.
Gleaming shards of love's own crime,
Capturing hearts, one breath at a time.

In the mirror, reflections taunt,
Memories haunt, like ghosts that daunt.
A dance of hope, of longing dreams,
In every glance, the silence screams.

Yet still we yearn, in twilight's glow,
For what we lost, the love we owe.
Despite the scars that mark our soul,
We strive to find, again, our whole.

Frozen Horizons of Distant Worlds

Beyond the reach of time and space,
Frozen horizons hold their grace.
Veils of ice, like whispering dreams,
Protect the tales of ancient themes.

Each flake that falls, a story told,
Of distant worlds, both fierce and bold.
In the silence, secrets sleep,
Guarded well, their promise deep.

Mountains rise in tranquil might,
Touching skies, a wondrous sight.
Winds enchant the snow-draped plains,
Echoing life's eternal strains.

Beneath the frost, where no light stirs,
Lies the heart of what was hers.
In frozen depths, emotions lie,
Burning still, like stars up high.

In search of warmth through icy veils,
We navigate these timeless trails.
For every step we take is bold,
In frozen worlds, our dreams unfold.

Luminous Mosaics under Arctic Skies

Across the canvas, colors blend,
Luminous mosaics never end.
Dancing lights in vibrant hues,
Paint the night with nature's muse.

Stars alight, like diamonds rare,
Fill the sky with wondrous flare.
Beneath the glow of aurora's song,
In this beauty, we belong.

The cold embraces, yet we feel,
A warmth that time cannot conceal.
Hearts ignite with fervent sparks,
Illuminating cosmic arcs.

In each breath, the magic swells,
As the Arctic's whisper tells.
Of dreams that chase the morning light,
Underneath the endless night.

So let the heavens cast their spell,
In this realm where wonders dwell.
Together, we'll explore the skies,
In luminous mosaics, love complies.

Whispers of Frosted Dreams

In the hush of winter's night,
Whispers float on silver light,
Dreams entwined with icy breath,
Softly crushing thoughts of death.

Beneath the stars, shadows play,
Chasing warmth from light of day,
Silent echoes drift and soar,
Yearning for what was before.

Winds caress the frosted trees,
Crystals glimmer in the freeze,
Nature's hush, a calming balm,
Wrapped in stillness, sweet and calm.

In the quiet, spirits blend,
Whimsical paths where dreams extend,
Carried forth on whispering winds,
To where every journey begins.

Hope emerges from the chill,
In the heart, a steady thrill,
Frosted dreams awaken bright,
Guided gently by the night.

Celestial Glimmers in Winter's Veil

Beneath the cosmic tapestry,
Stars are scattered effortlessly,
In winter's hush, their gentle glow,
Whispers secrets from below.

Snowflakes drift, a soft embrace,
Kissing earth in tranquil grace,
Each one's dance, a fleeting cheer,
Silent stories, crystal clear.

Cold winds weave through branches bare,
Framing dreams with care and flair,
Celestial glimmers shine above,
Stirring in the heart, sweet love.

In this night, the world is wide,
Magic sparks as stars collide,
Winter's veil, so pure and bright,
Wraps us in its tender light.

In the quiet, hopes arise,
Reflecting in the endless skies,
Life unfurls, a waking song,
Embracing all where we belong.

Moonlit Crystal Dance

Underneath the silver moon,
Nature hums a gentle tune,
Crystal shards in frosty air,
Dancing light, beyond compare.

Footprints trace on powdered ground,
Echoes of a soft, sweet sound,
Every step, a fleeting glance,
Inviting dreams to join the dance.

In the stillness, shadows play,
Whimsical in their own way,
Winds embrace, a lover's sigh,
Moonbeams twinkle in the sky.

Stars convene in radiant sway,
As night turns softly into day,
Time suspends, and hearts ignite,
Lost within the blissful night.

So let us twirl 'neath this spell,
Where every moment whispers well,
The moonlit journey, hand in hand,
In the magic, we will stand.

A Symphony of Chill

Whispers ride the frozen air,
As snowflakes dance without a care.
Each breath a cloud, a fleeting sight,
In winter's hold, the world feels right.

Crisp echoes in the still of night,
Stars above, a shimm'ring light.
Trees stand clad in white attire,
A tranquil frame, as dreams conspire.

Warmth within, yet cold outside,
Nature's beauty, winter's pride.
Fires crackle, shadows play,
In this chill, we find our way.

Footsteps crunch on frosty ground,
In silence, peace is truly found.
Time slows down, the world in pause,
A symphony of chill, because.

So let the winter tale unfold,
In stories shared and whispers bold.
The symphony of chill shall reign,
A soothing balm amidst the pain.

Winter's Celestial Gaze

Above, the moon, a silver sphere,
In winter's night, it shines so clear.
Stars align in frosty lace,
A celestial dance, a timeless grace.

Soft snow blankets the sleeping earth,
Whispers of peace, a quiet mirth.
The world transformed in timeless glow,
Under winter's gaze, dreams grow.

Crimson sunsets fade to night,
Golden dawns, a pure delight.
Every twinkle, a wish we send,
In winter's arms, our hearts shall mend.

Silhouettes of trees stand tall,
Guardians of the icy sprawl.
In their shadows, secrets weave,
In this winter, we believe.

Awake, the heart in frosty air,
As winter's gaze shows love and care.
Together we embrace the chill,
In winter's silence, time stands still.

Crystalline Nocturne

Underneath the starlit glow,
A crystalline blanket starts to flow.
Each flake a note, a song in flight,
Whispers of winter fill the night.

Moonlight sparkles on icy streams,
Rippling softly through the dreams.
Nature hums a lullaby sweet,
A nocturne played on frozen sheets.

Winter's breath, both sharp and clear,
Echoes soft in the atmosphere.
Every corner, a hidden spell,
In this silence, we dwell so well.

Gentle winds, a soft caress,
Wrap the world in gentle dress.
Stars dazzle in the velvet sky,
Under their watch, whispers sigh.

Awake we are, in frosty air,
In crystalline beauty, beyond compare.
The night unfolds, a tale untold,
In winter's magic, hearts behold.

Frosted Jewels

Glistening patterns on frosted glass,
Nature's artistry, a timeless class.
Each detail speaks of winter's charm,
In these jewels, there's no harm.

Icicles hang like crystal dreams,
Reflecting sunlight, softly gleams.
Every breath misting in the air,
A moment captured, pure and rare.

Through the trees, a chill wind blows,
Dancing lightly, it gently flows.
Leaves of silver, the world adorned,
In winter's grasp, our hearts are warmed.

Snowflakes tumble, each one unique,
Whispers of magic, so to speak.
In trails of white, we leave our mark,
Frosted jewels in the frozen dark.

So let us wander, hand in hand,
Through winter's wonder, a snowy land.
In every flake, a story spins,
In frosted jewels, the magic begins.

Midnight's Glow

In the stillness, shadows creep,
Stars appear, secrets deep.
A silver moon, softly bright,
Guides lost dreams through the night.

Whispers dance on cool night air,
Touching hearts with gentle care.
A world wrapped in quiet grace,
Magic lingers in this place.

Lost in thoughts that gently sway,
As time slips softly away.
Memories like fireflies roam,
In the dark, they find their home.

With every twinkle, stories wake,
Truths forgotten, hearts they stake.
In this hour, passions swell,
Midnight's glow casts its spell.

In the dawn, the whispers fade,
Yet in dreams, their serenade.
The night holds a timeless grace,
A fleeting, warm embrace.

Whispered Chills

Fog descends with muted sighs,
Beneath the weight of heavy skies.
Each breath a cloud, a ghostly wisp,
In the silence, shadows lisp.

Leaves rustle in the fading light,
Carrying tales from day to night.
Each whisper sends a shiver down,
A haunting tune, a spectral crown.

Trees loom tall, their branches bare,
Reaching out like fingers, rare.
The world breathes in this eerie chill,
Time stands still as dreams distill.

Cold winds dance through empty streets,
Where laughter fades, where silence greets.
In every corner, secrets cling,
Awakening the night to sing.

Yet in this strange, enchanted haze,
Life holds a beauty hard to praise.
Frosty tales, under stars, spill,
In the shadows, whispered chills.

Tides of Frost

A blanket white, the world transformed,
Winter's breath, all hearts warmed.
Tides of frost on panes arise,
Painting dreams 'neath heavy skies.

Footsteps crunching, echoes sound,
In the stillness, beauty found.
Glistening branches, bright and pure,
Nature's canvas, timeless, sure.

The rivers freeze, a glassy sheen,
Reflecting stars in dances keen.
Winter's kiss on each cheek laid,
In this moment, worries fade.

Snowflakes twirl like distant thoughts,
Weaving tales that time forgot.
Each flake unique, a story told,
In this wonder, hearts unfold.

As morning breaks, the sun does rise,
Chasing dreams across the skies.
In the light, the frost will melt,
But in hearts, its magic felt.

Beacon of the Night

A lone light flickers by the shore,
Guiding ships to safety's door.
In the dark, a promise shines,
Carving paths through fate's designs.

Waves crash softly, whispers call,
Echoes dance, a siren's thrall.
The beacon stands, both proud and free,
A guardian of the endless sea.

Stars align in cosmic grace,
Reflecting dreams in time and space.
Each flicker holds a tale untold,
In solitude, its heart unfolds.

Fog may roll, and shadows loom,
Yet its light dispels the gloom.
With every pulse, a vow it keeps,
Through tempest's fury, the lighthouse weeps.

As night surrenders to the dawn,
The beacon's light will still be drawn.
In every heart, its warmth ignites,
A steadfast hope, a guiding light.

Icebound Celestials

In stillness, stars collide,
Galaxies wrapped in white,
A shimmer on the frigid tide,
Frozen hands of night.

Veils of frost embrace the sky,
Whispers of the cosmic dance,
Light so soft, a distant sigh,
In this cold, we find romance.

Polar dreams in ice are cast,
Celestial fires burn so bright,
Through the ages, shadows last,
Guided by the starlit night.

Comets weave in frozen lace,
Their trails mark the quiet air,
In this vast and endless space,
A tapestry beyond compare.

Awake in dreams where cold prevails,
In the heart of winter's dome,
Among icebound celestials,
We find our forever home.

Frigid Radiance

Beneath a veil of crystal light,
Night unveils its icy charm,
Stars aglow in frosty flight,
Casting spells that softly warm.

Each flake glimmers from above,
A silent song of glacial grace,
In the still, we find our love,
Embracing time and frozen space.

The moon drapes silver on the land,
Illuminating paths so clear,
In this world, hand in hand,
Frigid radiance draws us near.

Shadows dance beneath the glow,
Echoes of a timeless seam,
In the night, the cold winds blow,
Whispering dreams that softly beam.

Together, we'll embrace the chill,
In the breath of winter's night,
With frigid radiance that will,
Guide us through the endless light.

Cosmic Patterns in the Snow

In the snow, a story traced,
Cosmic patterns, pure and bright,
Each flake holds a dream embraced,
Whispers of the endless night.

Footsteps echo, soft and slow,
Through this land of frosty grace,
In the magic of the snow,
We find our hidden place.

Celestial maps laid out below,
Coordinates of dreams untold,
With every step, our spirits flow,
In this world of shimmering cold.

Crystals shimmer in the dark,
A dance of light upon the ground,
Every breath, a fleeting spark,
In the silence, love is found.

So let us walk this path of white,
Where stars and snowflakes intertwine,
In cosmic patterns, pure delight,
Our hearts forever align.

Celestial Waltz on Crystal Shores

On crystal shores where shadows blend,
Celestial waltzes take their flight,
In the night, where dreams descend,
Starlit whispers fill the sight.

Waves of ice, so bold and clear,
Chanting songs of distant realms,
In the midst, we draw you near,
Guided by the stars' soft helms.

Each movement etched in frozen time,
Gracing dreams with silken glow,
In the dance, a rhythm prime,
Celestial secrets softly flow.

Together, under cosmic beams,
We twirl upon the glistening shore,
In this ballet, lost in dreams,
Forever longing to explore.

So let us waltz beneath the sky,
With hearts that shimmer, souls that soar,
On crystal shores, where we rely,
Celestial love forevermore.

A Dance of Shards

In the mirror's fractured light,
Colors twirl, a dazzling sight.
Each piece whispers, tales untold,
A symphony of dreams and gold.

Barefoot upon the glassy floor,
Hearts unite, then break once more.
Shimmering echoes fill the air,
Life's sharp edges laid bare.

Footsteps tracing paths of grace,
Every twirl a fleeting chase.
In the shards, we find our way,
Dancing through the light of day.

Tangled shadows, bright and clear,
Drawn together, held so near.
With each beat, the world expands,
As magic weaves in gentle hands.

Together, we defy the night,
In our hearts, a glowing light.
A dance upon the edges bright,
In the shattering, we take flight.

Celestial Glow

Underneath the vast, dark sky,
Stars are winking, low and high.
A blanket of dreams, soft and deep,
Whispers of the cosmos seep.

Moonlight dances on the lake,
Glistening waves that gently shake.
Each ripple tells a story bright,
Wrapped in warmth of silver light.

Comets streak with trails of fire,
Uplifting hopes, igniting desire.
Overhead, the heavens unfold,
In their splendor, secrets told.

Galaxies spin in an endless twirl,
A cosmic dance, a wondrous swirl.
Cradled in the universe's hand,
We reach towards the bright, unplanned.

With every breath, we feel the flow,
In infinity's embrace, we glow.
Journeying through the astral seam,
Lost within a starlit dream.

Frosted Starlings

In winter's grasp, the starlings fly,
Dark silhouettes against the sky.
A murmuration, wild and free,
Spinning tales of harmony.

They weave through branches, crisp and bare,
Frosty whispers fill the air.
Each flutter sings of chill and grace,
Nature's pulse in a silver embrace.

Beneath the clouds, shadows collide,
In patterns where secrets abide.
A dance of feathers, cold and bright,
Unfolds within the windowlight.

The frost bites soft upon the skin,
Yet the warmth of spirit flows within.
Together, they chase the twilight's thrill,
Frosted starlings, sweet, and still.

As daylight fades, their chorus calls,
Echoes through the evening halls.
In the stillness, magic sparks,
Starlings light the quiet parks.

Twilight Glimmer

Fading light in the evening sky,
Colors swirl as day waves goodbye.
Shadows lengthen, softly creep,
As the world drifts into sleep.

Golden hues begin to wane,
In the stillness, peace remains.
Stars peek out, a shy debut,
Painting dreams in twilight's hue.

The horizon glows, ablaze with grace,
Whispers echo in twilight's embrace.
Nature's palette, a gentle blend,
Marks the day's sweet, tender end.

In the hush, a secret spun,
Night unfolds, the day is done.
Each flicker tells a tale anew,
In the twilight, dreams ensue.

The moon ascends, a silver ball,
Bold and luminous, over all.
Guiding hearts with its soft glow,
In the twilight, magic flows.

Radiant Chill

In winter's grasp, the world does pause,
A sparkling hush, where silence draws.
The breath of night, so crisp, so clear,
A radiant chill, the heart held near.

Stars above, they twinkle bright,
In this cold, a soft delight.
The moonlight weaves through icy trees,
As whispers float upon the breeze.

Snowflakes dance on gentle air,
Each flake a wish, a silent prayer.
Beneath the frost, the earth does sleep,
In radiant chill, our dreams do leap.

A moment caught in twilight's frame,
Where crystal hues ignite the flame.
With every breath, the world exhales,
In glistening night, beauty prevails.

Whispers of warmth in shadows blend,
As daylight's touch begins to mend.
Yet, still we cherish winter's song,
In radiant chill, where hearts belong.

Cosmic Crystals

In the night sky, crystals gleam,
Galaxies swirl in a dream.
Each star, a gem, in velvet deep,
A cosmic dance that stirs our sleep.

Through cosmic winds, the currents flow,
Mysteries vast, forever grow.
Nebulae bloom, colors ignite,
Painting the canvas of endless night.

Every twinkle, a story told,
In the silence, the universe unfolds.
Constellations map our fate,
Cosmic crystals, we contemplate.

Around us, time begins to bend,
As stardust trails, worlds blend.
In this expanse, we find our place,
Cosmic crystals, infinite grace.

Between the folds of space and time,
We reach for dreams, and stars that climb.
In the heart of night, we stake our claim,
In cosmic crystals, we are the same.

Shimmering Shadows

In the twilight, colors fade,
Shimmering shadows softly laid.
A dance of light, the dusk's embrace,
Whispers linger, a tranquil space.

Through the trees, the breezes sigh,
As day retreats, and night draws nigh.
Moonbeams flicker on the ground,
In shimmering shadows, peace is found.

Echoes of laughter, memories low,
Reflections of moments, ebb and flow.
In the hush where secrets dwell,
Shimmering shadows weave their spell.

With every step, the night unveils,
Stories told by the gentle gales.
Where light and dark in harmony fade,
In shimmering shadows, dreams are laid.

As stars awaken from their rest,
We find solace in the crest.
With open hearts, we embrace the night,
In shimmering shadows, we ignite.

Ethereal Frost

In dawn's embrace, the world aglow,
An ethereal frost, a crystal show.
Branches wear their diamond crowns,
Nature's splendor, in silent towns.

A magical touch on fields of white,
Where whispers linger, soft and light.
Through every breath, a dream's caress,
An ethereal frost, pure and blessed.

Under the sun's first gentle rays,
The frost glimmers, in a daze.
Each flake a wonder, each glint a gleam,
In this moment, life feels like a dream.

Nature's canvas painted bright,
With frosty hues, a pure delight.
In stillness found, beneath this frost,
In every sparkle, we find what's lost.

As day unfolds, the frost will fade,
But memories linger in light's cascade.
In the heart of winter, we find our trust,
In ethereal frost, we feel the rush.

The Frozen Firmament

Stars twinkle in a veil of ice,
Whispers of dreams, a silent slice.
Moonlight glimmers on snowflakes rare,
In this stillness, I find my prayer.

Breath of winter chills the night,
Painting shadows, a crystal light.
Beneath the cosmos, the world sleeps,
In the cold, the heart still keeps.

Through the silence, a gentle breeze,
Carrying tales from frozen seas.
Echoes of ages long since past,
In this firmament, time's hold is vast.

Nights stretch out like endless seas,
In the hush, the soul finds ease.
Among the stars, I wander free,
In the frost, my spirit sees.

Awake to the stillness all around,
Where serenity in silence is found.
Each twinkling light, a guiding spark,
In the frozen firmament, love leaves its mark.

Light Beyond the Glacier

Beneath the weight of ice so blue,
Shimmers of sunlight break on through.
A dance of hues, the morning wakes,
With warmth that melts, the stillness breaks.

Silent vistas stretch wide and vast,
Memories catch in the shadows cast.
In the heart of winter, hope still grows,
In nature's grasp, the magic flows.

Reflections shimmer on icy streams,
Flowing gently like whispered dreams.
The promise of spring in the air,
Awakens the world with fragrant care.

Traces of warmth, a gentle tease,
As glaciers sigh with the softest breeze.
Light dances through the frozen land,
Unfolding beauty, a guiding hand.

In the embrace of crystal skies,
Where every heartache slowly dies.
Beyond the glacier, life will reign,
In the light, the soul finds gain.

Cosmic Frostbite

In the void where silence reigns,
Frostbitten dreams hold fragile chains.
Stars flicker, a haunting sight,
In the cosmos' chill, a silent fight.

Cold winds whisper ancient tales,
Of distant worlds and icy gales.
They weave the fabric of time and fate,
In the frozen expanse, we contemplate.

Galaxies drift in a starry sea,
Each spark of light calls out to me.
Through the frost, I yearn to fly,
To break the chains and touch the sky.

Yet each cold breath feels like flame,
A cosmic dance with no two the same.
In the frostbite, I find my truth,
A timeless echo, the voice of youth.

So here I stand, on this cosmic edge,
With whispers of light, I find my pledge.
In the cold embrace of night's delight,
I carve my path in the starlit light.

Glacial Radiance

In the dawn of winter's breath,
Glacial radiance hints of death.
Yet in the cold, a beauty wakes,
A shimmer soft, a heart that shakes.

Mountains rise in robes of white,
Against the sky, a wondrous sight.
Reflecting light, the ice will gleam,
In this landscape, lost in dream.

Beneath the surface, life persists,
Amidst the frost, the spirit twists.
Each flake that falls, a silent song,
In this realm where we belong.

Rays of sunshine break the gloom,
Chasing shadows, dispelling doom.
Glacial radiance warms the soul,
In winter's grasp, we find our whole.

So let us dance in frozen light,
A harmony in the darkest night.
Through glacial beauty, we shall see,
The warmth of love in eternity.

Glimmering Paths

Through the trees, the light does dance,
A sparkling trail, a fleeting chance.
Footsteps whisper on the ground,
In nature's embrace, peace is found.

Golden rays in morning dew,
Each step bright, feels fresh and new.
Shadows stretch as daylight fades,
While secrets hide in forest glades.

Winding routes call out my name,
Each turn a spark, each moment's flame.
A journey painted with delight,
Guided softly by the light.

Leaves rustle with ancient tales,
As twilight set, adventure hails.
Stars awaken, the night is clear,
I wander on, without a fear.

With every glimmer, dreams unfold,
Paths of promise, stories told.
In the heart of woods so deep,
Glimmering paths where spirits leap.

Boreal Secrets

In the hush of the pine-clad night,
Whispers float beneath starlight.
Ancient trees, stoic and wise,
Guard the secrets of the skies.

Frozen streams like crystal veins,
Carry echoes of silent pains.
The moon drapes silver on the ground,
While nightingales sing, profound.

Shadows shift with a playful grace,
In this stillness, we find our place.
Nature's breath, a gentle sigh,
In the boreal, dreams drift by.

Beneath the frost, the earth sleeps tight,
Hoping for the warmth of light.
Hushed lullabies of winter's hold,
Secrets worth their weight in gold.

In the woods where spirits blend,
Boreal secrets never end.
With every thrum of nature's song,
We are reminded: we belong.

Echoes in the Snow

Silent flakes on a canvas white,
Every hush a pure delight.
Footsteps leave a temporary trace,
In winter's serene and quiet space.

Whispers carried on the breeze,
Through branches bare, the frost-laden trees.
Voices echo, a timeless sound,
In the stillness of the ground.

Stars cascade from the heavens above,
Sending peace, and warmth, and love.
Each flurry holds a story old,
In the silence, secrets unfold.

Night descends with a velvet touch,
Cradling all, it means so much.
An enchanted world wrapped tight,
Echoes linger in the night.

As dawn breaks with a gentle glow,
We treasure each soft, white shadow.
Moments whispered, choices flowed,
In echoes of the snow, we've strode.

Diamonds in the Frost

A breath of winter enchants the air,
With each exhale, beauty laid bare.
In the early light, the sparkles gleam,
Nature's jewels, a frozen dream.

Crystalline patterns form on the ground,
Each moment precious, peace surrounds.
Sunrise paints diamonds in their glow,
Whispers of magic in the snow.

Branches laden, a silvery lace,
A fleeting wonder, a soft embrace.
The world aglow with chilly delight,
In the hush, every heart takes flight.

As shadows lengthen, the day unwinds,
A quiet retreat, solace it finds.
In the twilight, reflections ignite,
Diamonds twinkle, merging with night.

Amidst the frost, dreams softly weave,
In this beauty, we learn to believe.
Each challenge faced, like ice, we defrost,
In love's embrace, we find what we've lost.

Frost-kissed Dreams

In the quiet of the night,
Whispers dance on frozen air.
Stars hang like distant lights,
Painting dreams beyond compare.

Snowflakes twirl in gentle grace,
Caressing every sleeping tree.
Crystals glimmer, softly trace,
A world wrapped in mystery.

Moonlight bathes the silent hills,
A silver cloak on nature's heart.
Each breath reveals the planet's thrills,
Frosted beauty, a work of art.

Beneath the chill, warmth still remains,
Hope blooms as the dawn draws near.
Frost-kissed dreams like soft refrains,
Whispering secrets we hold dear.

Embrace the glow, the fleeting light,
For spring will soon disperse the cold.
In every shadow, a hint of bright,
Frost-kissed tales yet to be told.

Echoes of the Cosmos

In the vastness of the night,
Stars compose a tranquil song.
Galaxies spin, a wondrous sight,
Whispers of where we all belong.

Nebulae cradle dreams in hues,
Colors blending, bright and deep.
Every twinkle, a tale to choose,
In the cosmos, secrets sleep.

Planets dance in silent waltz,
Each orbit a rhythm so divine.
Infinite space, no faults,
The universe, a grand design.

Radiant echoes fill the void,
Messages from the past arise.
Curiosity, never destroyed,
In starlit wonder, all must rise.

So under this celestial dome,
Let our hearts seek out the bright.
In echoes of the cosmos roam,
Finding dreams in endless night.

Shattered Reflections

Fragments of a broken past,
Mirrors cracked, yet still they show.
Fleeting moments, shadows cast,
In the shards, our tales they flow.

Each piece holds a whispered sigh,
Memories where light once danced.
In the chaos, a reason why,
Life's journey, beautifully enhanced.

Through the cracks, a light breaks through,
Illuminating what's been lost.
Grow from pain, learn what's true,
Embrace the past, no matter the cost.

Shattered, yet we find our way,
Picking up the scattered dreams.
In the light of a new day,
From broken, vibrant hope redeems.

So let the fragments tell the tale,
Of resilience, love, and grace.
In shattered reflections, we prevail,
Finding strength in every space.

Radiance Adrift

Waves of light upon the sea,
Dancing gently with the breeze.
Radiance calls, wild and free,
In the depths, our spirits tease.

Each shimmer tells a story new,
Of journeys taken far and wide.
In the currents, dreams pursue,
With every tide, our hearts abide.

Castles made of sun and sand,
Fleeting as the ocean's sighs.
A world shaped by nature's hand,
Where the shore meets endless skies.

Drifting onward, time unfolds,
Seagulls follow, weaving grace.
In the radiance, we behold,
Moments captured, time and space.

So when the sun begins to set,
And colors dance in twilight's kiss,
Let every memory be your net,
For in this radiance, find your bliss.

Ethereal Beacons in the Cold

In the stillness, shadows dance,
Whispers of light in a trance.
Stars flicker like secrets untold,
Ethereal beacons in the cold.

Softly they sway, a ghostly tune,
Painting the night with silver moon.
Paths illuminated, a guide they hold,
Ethereal beacons in the cold.

Frosted breath in the midnight air,
Glimmers of beauty, beyond compare.
In frozen realms, the dreams unfold,
Ethereal beacons in the cold.

Nature sighs, her canvas bright,
Stars awaken with gentle light.
Fleeting moments, a story retold,
Ethereal beacons in the cold.

Together they rise, a shimmering glow,
Guiding lost souls in the snow.
In this magic, we find our hold,
Ethereal beacons in the cold.

Chilled Luminescence

In the heart of winter's night,
Softly shines a gentle light.
Crystals twinkle, dreams unspooled,
Chilled luminescence, pure and cooled.

Beneath the stars, the silence sings,
A blanket of frost, the joy it brings.
Glows of white like memories pooled,
Chilled luminescence, pure and cooled.

Winds caress the frozen ground,
In this magic, peace is found.
Breath of winter, soft and ruled,
Chilled luminescence, pure and cooled.

Glistening paths where footsteps fade,
Each flicker tells a tale displayed.
In tranquil scenes, our hearts are schooled,
Chilled luminescence, pure and cooled.

As dawn brushes the night away,
Yonder, the warmth begins to play.
Golden hues in beauty schooled,
Chilled luminescence, pure and cooled.

Aurora's Embrace on Shimmering Snow

Beyond the horizon, colors collide,
Aurora's dance in the evening tide.
Ripples of light in the softest glow,
Aurora's embrace on shimmering snow.

With every wave, the heavens sway,
Strokes of brilliance, fading gray.
Nature whispers in tones that flow,
Aurora's embrace on shimmering snow.

In the quiet, frozen and fair,
Dreams awaken, floating in air.
Beneath the stars, a magical show,
Aurora's embrace on shimmering snow.

Night wraps softly, a silken shroud,
Whispers of color, vibrant and loud.
In the stillness, hearts aglow,
Aurora's embrace on shimmering snow.

Together we stand, hand in hand,
Enthralled by the wonder across the land.
In this moment, time feels slow,
Aurora's embrace on shimmering snow.

Glittering Nightscapes

In the velvet of night, stars gleam,
Over valleys, a whispering dream.
Nature's canvas, a grand tableau,
Glittering nightscapes steal the show.

Mountains rise with a frosty crown,
Silhouettes deep in shadows drown.
Beneath the cosmos, we ebb and flow,
Glittering nightscapes steal the show.

With every flicker, stories unfold,
A tapestry woven with wonders bold.
Beneath the shimmer, we come to know,
Glittering nightscapes steal the show.

In tranquil hours, the heart takes flight,
As dreams ignite in the still of night.
In twilight's hold, the magic will grow,
Glittering nightscapes steal the show.

Hand in hand, through silence we glide,
Lost in the beauty, side by side.
In these moments, love's gentle glow,
Glittering nightscapes steal the show.

Twinkling Dreams Beneath the Skies

Stars whisper softly, night glows bright,
Dreams take flight, in the quiet light.
Clouds gently drift, secrets unfold,
Under the cosmos, hearts turn bold.

Wishes are painted, silver and blue,
Every twinkle, a promise anew.
Gentle breezes weave through the trees,
Melodies carried, brought by the pleas.

Moments suspended, in time's embrace,
Laughter and joy, dance in this space.
Distant horizons, beckon the soul,
Filling the night, making us whole.

In the twilight, dreams intertwine,
Fleeting shadows, entwined with the divine.
Hope glimmers brightly, a guiding star,
In twinkling dreams, we wander afar.

Infinite stories among the stars,
Opening doors to mysteries ours.
Beneath the skies, we find our way,
In twinkling dreams, forever stay.

Frosted Wishes on Glacial Winds

Beneath the frost, whispers do call,
Wishes rise up, from winters' thrall.
Glacial winds carry dreams so bright,
In frosty breath, they take to flight.

Icicles glimmer, like jewels they gleam,
In the cold air, there lives a dream.
Frozen rivers sing a soft tune,
Echoes of heart in the cold afternoon.

Snowflakes dancing, a delicate swirl,
Whirling wishes in a gentle whirl.
Crystals adorn the branches' embrace,
Painting the landscape, a white lace grace.

Through icy paths, we wander and roam,
Frosted wishes find their way home.
As glacial winds weave through the night,
In the still air, our hopes ignite.

Together we dream as the cold winds blow,
Frosted wishes in moonlight's glow.
Each breath a whisper, each sigh a flight,
In the chill of winter, we find our light.

Chilled Echoes of Hidden Wonders

In the stillness, echoes unfold,
Whispers of wonders, secrets untold.
Chilled air carries a haunting sound,
In hidden corners, magic is found.

Shadows linger, playing their game,
Fleeting glimpses tease and tame.
Mysteries dwell, waiting to share,
Chilled echoes dance in the midnight air.

With every rustle, stories arise,
Tales of enchantment beneath the skies.
Hushed breaths beckon the curious heart,
In the depths of night, we find our part.

Luminous glories, hidden from sight,
In every chill, a spark of light.
Chilled echoes linger, tales intertwine,
Whispers of wonders are solely mine.

The night unfolds, secrets amassed,
Through chilled echoes, we wander past.
In hushed allure, our dreams explore,
Hidden wonders, forevermore.

Ethereal Crystals of the Night

Moonlit glimmers dance on the ground,
Ethereal crystals, magic profound.
Under the stars, a secret unfold,
Reflections shimmer, stories retold.

A tapestry woven with silver and gray,
Crystals of night lead the weary astray.
Each brilliant spark, a fleeting embrace,
In the still shadows, we find our place.

The night sky drapes like a velvet cloth,
Whispering tales as we softly troth.
Ethereal wonders pulse in the dark,
Waiting and watching, like a hidden spark.

With every breath, a dream takes flight,
Crystals gleam softly, embracing the night.
Under the gaze of a luminous moon,
We grasp at marvels, a timeless tune.

In quiet moments, all worries dissolve,
Ethereal crystals, our hearts evolve.
In the magic of night, together we play,
Finding our dreams beneath skies' array.

Milton Keynes UK
Ingram Content Group UK Ltd.
UKHW010229111224
452348UK00011B/624